CLUB Q

CLUB Q

JAMES DAVIS

WAYWISER

First published in 2020 by

THE WAYWISER PRESS

Christmas Cottage, Church Enstone, Chipping Norton, Oxfordshire, OX7 4NN, UK
P.O. Box 6205, Baltimore, MD 21206, USA
https://waywiser-press.com

Editor-in-Chief
Philip Hoy

Senior American Editor
Joseph Harrison

Associate Editors
Eric McHenry | Dora Malech | V. Penelope Pelizzon | Clive Watkins
Greg Williamson | Matthew Yorke

Copyright © James Davis, 2020

The right of James Davis to be identified as the author of this work
has been asserted by him in accordance with the
Copyright, Designs and Patents Act of 1988.

All rights reserved. No part of this publication may be reproduced, stored in
a retrieval system, or transmitted in any form or by any means, electronic,
mechanical, photocopying, recording, or otherwise, without the prior permission
of both the copyright owner and the above publisher of this book.

9 7 5 3 1 2 4 6 8

A CIP catalogue record for this book is available from the British Library.

ISBN 978-1-911379-01-0

Printed and bound by
T. J. International Ltd., Padstow, Cornwall, PL28 8RW

for Hope, my mother

Acknowledgments

The author wishes to thank the following publications, in which versions of some of these poems first appeared:

8 Poems: "Ax"
32 Poems: "Shout to the Lord"
American Literary Review: "Teaching a Gay Poem"
The Berkshire Eagle: "Ba," "Ta"
Best New Poets 2011: "Aa"
Best New Poets 2019: "In Houston"
Copper Nickel: "American Gothic"
Cream City Review: "Personal"
Defenestration: "Ab"
The Fourth River: "Club Q," "Gainesville Sestina," "The Weekend After"
Gargoyle: "We Are the World" (as "Charity")
The Gay & Lesbian Review: "Bi"
Hobart: "Arcade-Scented Candle," "Faith"
HTMLGiant: "Spiritual Warfare"
Inverted Syntax: "Al," "An," "Ar"
Measure: "Episode 60"
Nimrod: "As," "Ex"
Otoliths: "This Poem Is So Middle-Class, It's Pathetic"
Pebble Lake Review: "Heart Smart" (as "They're Great")

"To the Observant Motorist Who Called Me Faggot" was selected as the Goodreads Poem of the Month for June 2009 and appeared in the Goodreads.com newsletter.

"State of the Union" is after Jericho Brown's "Homeland." "Between *Home and Sexual*" is after Tony Hoagland's "Hearings." "Self-Portrait as Articulated Wall" is after Herbert Bayer's sculpture *articulated wall*. Much of the language in "Spiritual Warfare" is taken from Adam Lamontagne's walkthrough of the NES game *Spiritual Warfare* on gamefaqs.com. The opening of "Magnavox Opus" is an adaptation of the opening of Eavan Boland's "The Parcel."

Some of these poems were written under the auspices of the Lighthouse

Acknowledgments

Writers Workshop's Poetry Collective and The Mastheads Writers' Residency.

Thanks to my writing teachers, especially Tony Hoagland, Debora Greger, William Logan, Michael Hofmann, Sidney Wade, Elizabeth Robinson, Andrea Rexilius, Terrance Hayes, and Carolina Ebeid, whose instruction helped produce much of the work in this collection. Deepest gratitude to Ed Hirsch for selecting *Club Q* for the Hecht Prize.

Special thanks to Amanda Curry, Donal Mosher, Emily Pérez, Eric Smith, and Laura Paul Watson for their help editing and ordering the poems in this manuscript. And finally, thanks to my poetry cohort at the University of Florida—Diya Chaudhuri, Laura Deily, Jessica Hammack, and Karin Lightstone—for being an inexhaustible source of joy and frolic.

Contents

FOREWORD BY EDWARD HIRSCH ... xi

Quest

Shout to the Lord	3
The Dunes	4
Faith	5
This Poem Is So Middle-Class, It's Pathetic	6
Personal	7
Murray	8
In Houston	9
Spiritual Warfare	10
Joel	11
Club Q	12
Mega Man	13
The Human Situation	15
Heart Smart	17
Stick to the Subject	18
We Are the World	19
Gainesville Sestina	20
Heaven's Gates, Hell's Flames	22
The Weekend After	24
Arcade-Scented Candle	25
The Hobbyist	26

Queries

Aa	31
Ab	32
Al	33
An	34
Ar	35
As	36
Ax	37

Ba	38
Bi	39
El	40
Em	41
Ex	42
Ha	43
Id	44
Is	45
Om	47
Qi	49
Ta	50
Us	56
Za	57

QUOTIDIAN

State of the Union	61
American Gothic	62
Unmentionables	63
To the Observant Motorist Who Called Me Faggot	64
Bingo	65
gay4pay	68
Teaching a Gay Poem	69
Dating My Mom	70
White Chickens	71
Lemmings	72
Magnavox Opus	73
Episode 60	75
Self-Portrait as Articulated Wall	76
Sincerely, Chipotle	77
Agate	83
Diaristic	85
This Poem Is a Gift to Myself	86
A Brief History of the Denver Scrabble Club	87

Contents

Between *Home* and *Sexual*   89

A Note about the Author   91

A Note about the Anthony Hecht Poetry Prize   93

Foreword by Edward Hirsch

Club Q is a startling book. It is cleverly conceived, formally deft, musically resourceful. It is also flamboyantly gay, the queerest of queer poetry books—it keeps finding closets to shred—and takes special pleasure in its literary outings and exposures, its urban scenes and outposts. I like the way it nods to Wallace Stevens and James Merrill, who claimed that he was "as American as lemon chiffon pie," and takes wordplay at its word, mining the language to see what it will yield. Here, "The Comedian as the Letter C" becomes the adventures of the letter *Q*, and a Gay poetic springs to life.

James Davis loves shimmering surfaces, linguistic games. But his virtuoso formal strategies only partly succeed in hiding the pain of a lonely, misunderstood childhood growing up in Colorado Springs, Colorado, dogged by malls and megachurches, shadowed by a U. S. Military base. Fundamentally speaking, evangelical Christian soldiers are everywhere. The first poem, "Shout to the Lord," starts the book off with a memory of being in church:

> What I know, at eight, of God:
> hymns on giant television screens,
> my father's tongues, and Sunday jeans,
> his sneakers on his hands. God,
>
> shrink me ten sizes. Wrap me in a bubble
> and let me float through the rafters,
> the spotlights, the flags of the distant cultures
> we pray for, here, inside our holy bubble.

The brightness of the form doesn't conceal the child's discomfort and desperation, his deep desire to float free and escape the godly bubble. So, too, the second poem, "The Dunes," provides an indelible portrait of the poet as a sensitive younger brother:

> The older brother throws rocks at the sparrows.
> That's what boys are supposed to do.
> The younger brother sits in tears,
> in protest, under a lone cottonwood.

Foreword by Edward Hirsch

In this book, we can trace some of the ways that a misfit kid who once sat in tears in silent protest grows up to become a gay man looking for a way to transcend his isolation and find community. He seeks a refuge. That's why *Q* becomes a *Club*.

Club Q is a heavily determined book, strategically divided into three sections: "Quest," "Queries," and "Quotidian." The letter *Q* in LGBTQ stands both for "gay" and for "questioning," and Davis uses it both ways in the title poem, which begins, "I stand for quest." He runs through various words beginning with the seventeenth letter of the alphabet, such as *queen* and *quarters*, and then homes in: "Of course, I stand / for queer. Which is to say unique, / which is to say alone." He soon picks up *quarantine* and *questioning*. In this poem and section of the book, the identification of the words leads outward to an identification of the experiences growing up and coming of age as an outsider trying to find a place for himself. "My father cried when I came out to him," he reports in his self-conscious lyric, "This Poem Is So Middle-Class, It's Pathetic," "It was at Jason's Deli. I handed him a serviette / and piled my salad bowl high with artichoke hearts." Here, the banality of the surroundings heightens the inarticulate pain of the encounter, the intimate relationship.

James Davis obviously plays a competitive game of Scrabble. Every poem in the second section of the book, "Queries," is titled after an unlikely word from *The Official SCRABBLE Player's Dictionary*, which he keeps close at hand. My sisters like to play Scrabble, and they often mock me because I can't resist plunking down the four-letter word, *poet*, which nets me a mere six points. Davis is smarter than that and plays for higher stakes. He uses the arbitrary nature of Scrabble to revel in the materiality of language. He probes obscure, often antique words, such as *Aa* ("rough, cindery lava"), which he likens to "America / with the middle part blacked out," and *Ta* ("an expression of gratitude"), which leads him to address God, whom he thanks "for existing and not existing," and to praise Scrabble, "for the words—the glorious, copious words." These poems glory in words so much that they become strange again.

The third section, "Quotidian," treats America in an ordinary, everyday way. It begins with a playful poem called "State of the Union" ("No one in America is healthy") and goes on to describe various uncomfortable situations and seemingly unmentionable subjects. America can be an extremely toxic place, especially for anyone who values difference, and Davis tends to deal with hateful language, hurtful subjects, at one remove, treating everything as a linguistic event. One example is the poem, "To the Observant Motorist Who Called Me Faggot." Here, he defangs the driver's insult by calling him "observant," and responds with the recognition, "We have names for things we barely understand." It's typical of him to repurpose and break down the smear: "I'm sure we both / can appreciate the way it splits // a word in two clean syllables: / the fag from it, the it from fag. // I like to think of myself as a hyphen."

Some of Davis's poems are American Gothics, others are self-portraits ("Teaching a Gay Poem," "Self-Portrait as an Articulated Wall"). The last poem, "Between *Home* and *Sexual*," is dedicated to Tony Hoagland, and one feels Hoagland's influence throughout this section, which has a sassy, vernacular, edgy way of thinking about mass culture. But it also has a deep undertow of concern for the vulnerable: "It's easy to forget / hatred never stops coming for any of us. / But hatred never stop coming for any of us." Yet Davis is remarkable in the way he responds to this bitter truth not just with outrage, but also with a counterweight of joie de vivre. The book ends with a recognition and prayer:

> Still summer, still the day I was born,
> and here by the river
> my fellow man is naked,
> pale, and, for the moment, safe
> as so many aren't. Soon,
> we will swim back into the water
> and together, hopefully, make it back to shore.

James Davis has a fresh voice and a witty, inclusive mission, and it gives me great pleasure to welcome this book into the world. I'm eager to invite you to a new democratic venue, which is now open: *Club Q*.

Quest

Shout to the Lord

What I know, at eight, of God:
hymns on giant television screens,
my father's tongues and Sunday jeans,
his sneakers on his hands. God,

shrink me ten sizes. Wrap me in a bubble
and let me float through the rafters,
the spotlights, the flags of the distant cultures
we pray for, here, inside our holy bubble.

It's easy, here, to believe in Jesus.
In the aisle, a man facedown on the carpet,
sobbing, his back heaving. *The Holy Spirit,*
my father says, *is pretty cool.* Jesus,

do I have to stand for two more hours?
Would it kill you if I sat down?
I ask my father if I may use the restroom,
where I'll try to spend the next two hours

reading my picture Bible in a stall:
the first day, the second, the third,
the fourth, the Fall, the Flood
inside the eight-square-cubit stall.

I'm afraid of hell. I count the tiles.
A speaker pipes in the choir, a song
I know by heart. The voices ring
off fifty thousand turquoise tiles.

The Dunes

The older brother throws rocks at the sparrows.
That's what boys are supposed to do.
The younger brother sits in tears,
in protest, under a lone cottonwood.

That's what boys are supposed to do
when innocents suffer. His father says
this protest under the lonely cottonwood
is evidence of weakness. Be strong

when innocents suffer, his father says.
The dunes are purpling like a bruise,
evidence of weakness. Strength is
a foundation of stone, not sand.

The dunes are blacker than a bruise.
The stepmother's pimento cheese
is a foundation of stone. Her sand-
wiches are unpleasant but serve their purpose.

The stepmother's pimento cheese
refuses to leave. It lasts for days,
which are unpleasant but serve their purpose.
The family eats in silence in their camper,

refusing to leave, their last days
eaten in the silent camper.
The older brother throws rocks at the sparrows.
The younger brother sits in tears.

Faith

The first time I opened my eyes during prayer,
the first thing I saw, across the table,
was my brother's stare, his thin grin,
his thick black eyebrows raised as if to say
what took you so long. Curiosity
is the recognition of ignorance
as a kind of sickness. My brother
broke the agreement he made with my father:
stop skipping church
and you can keep your bedroom door.
We woke Sunday morning to the power drill.

This Poem Is So Middle-Class, It's Pathetic

My mother has a word for what she's been doing since the Sixties:
piddling (verb, intransitive). We lick the rims of our margaritas, mine
    salted, hers sugared.

Fruity Pebbles, Hungry Man, everything I ate had a name
more memorable than mine. I am pretty good at a lot of things.

My obsession with thrift stores began in the ninth grade, a symptom of
my obsession with death. I wore a Number-One Grandpa sweatshirt. My
    mother threw it out.

As a rule, the middle class dances worse than both the upper and lower
    classes.
No pain moves us, nor have we been trained at imitating pain. This pains
    us.

Remember the night we held each other for the first time, how I collapsed
    into your body?
What a regrettable haircut I had. Why didn't you say something?

There's nothing sadder than a sad person who cannot clearly articulate
    his sadness.
I hope this poem is over soon. It's not going nearly as well as I
    anticipated.

My father cried when I came out to him. It was at a Jason's Deli. I
    handed him a serviette
and piled my salad bowl high with artichoke hearts.

Personal

Give me a faggot, fashion mags evenly fanned
across his coffee table, who serves drinks
in snifters, tumblers, flutes, and says *behind*,

not to euphemize *ass*, but to signal his nearing,
e.g. on a bike. Give me a man like an otter,
svelte swimmer with claws to tear flesh from pink

varicellate shells, fur matted with saltwater.
I want a mouth wet with philosophy,
lips slick with persuasion, a beard like my father's.

I want him to cook Sunday brunches for me:
eggs Benedict, Bloody Marys, metaphors
for the morning, for the health of our country.

Let us zinc our noses and tube down a river
on psilocybin. Let the summer burn us blond
right down to the pubes. Let desire

italicize our somberest sentiments: *there's sand
down my swimsuit.* And when the green day
ages into night, give us a patch of damp ground

under the mucilaginous Milky Way—
some plot of earth that does not care how we have sinned—
and we will be more than *cocksucker* implies.

Murray

My arrowgrass shot
straight into his burning pine.
His burning pine
set my bitterbush aflame.

> Our academy was nectar, an alarming vector.
> Together we assembled
> a downywood dreamcatcher.

Enough of Memorial Park,
he said. On to Cascade Avenue!
On to Bijou Boulevard!
On to Purgatory Drive!

> In time, his branding iron left a deep meridian
> in my limberwood galley.
> He felt carefree. I felt a saddle horn.

It must have been at the aeroplaza
when I slipped off his jetwing.
Or was it Constitution?
Or was it Stetson Hills?

> I got lost in his contrails.
> I think his name
> was Murray.

In Houston

Remembering it is like remembering the womb.
The heat. The concrete. The tofu sandwiches.

I was democratic there. I had directions in three languages.
I was punched in a Fiesta Mart parking lot. I was rigged.

I made out with hipsters, some of them straight,
all of them strangers, at a Seventies sportswear party.

Later, one told me, "You're right, MySpace
is for fascists and faggots, of which you are both."

I dabbled in Montrose and Montaigne, snorted half a line
behind the dumpster behind Texas Art Supply.

My French professor complimented my nasals.
Saint Barthélemy, she helped me say. *Sandbar tail me*.

There were the minor drugs: Adderall, cowboy killers, ironic
Tab. I was a sanctimonious double major. I learned

how things went bad. Potatoes liquefied in my pantry.
During the library renovations, I snuck classmates

up to the empty eighth floor and fingered their assholes.
How juvenile, my quest for omniscience.

Spiritual Warfare

*– for the Nintendo Entertainment System,
by Wisdom Tree, Inc., 1991, unlicensed*

Your enemies are not killed; they are converted.
Occasionally, a convert will drop Spirit Points,
which you can use to purchase things like fruits.

Each fruit has its own unique method of attack.
Pears, though weak, come in handy in the Slums
since they can destroy large weeds and junk piles.

Vials of the Wrath of God: these are basically bombs,
acquired in groups of three or seven. Samson's Jawbone
acts as a boomerang. You'll need this to get the Raft.

To begin, enter the red door and receive an apple
from the Christian Helper. The basketball player
you come across in the Park is of no consequence.

Do *not* go into the Bar in the Shipyard; you will lose
the Belt of Truth and have to go to the Pawn Shop
in the Slums to retrieve it. Using the Raft, cross the lake

and search out the Gray-Haired Man in the Airport.
He is slow and weak; it takes only three Vials
to convert him. He will drop the Helmet of Salvation,

which renders you invulnerable to dynamite.
Once you have obtained the banana, pass through the Woods
and enter the Prison, under which lies the Demon Stronghold.

The demons are vulnerable only to the banana.
You will soon be in a black room with the Demon Master.
He can be defeated with persistence. You will know

you have damaged him when his color flashes from red
to a lighter red—an almost imperceptible change.

Joel

His living room smelled clean as aspirin,
its bare white light bulbs haloed by thin smoke.
Nineteen, a dilettante, I'd burned his crystal.
A bitter crème-brûlée skin clogged the pipe.
He boiled the tar with a lighter's pinprick flame
and taught me how to shotgun, stubble pressed
against my peach-fuzzed lips, one fumy breath
reflating us until we cracked and kissed.

Fired from his job in Washington, he moved
back home, sold tina to Houston queens, bleach-blond
rednecks, their faces sucked into their skulls.
They flirted, took their Ziploc bags, and left.
He captained his LGBT softball team,
a hardy mix of sporty dykes and daddies,
their honors students texting in the stands.
His viral load stayed low; his pecs stayed high.

"Rubbeth my fat cock against thine arse,"
he told me once he'd gotten me in bed.
I'd told him I was majoring in English.
He said he wrote a poem once, an ode
to a twink he topped and then, too spun to sleep,
cleaned his whole apartment overnight.
The last line: "Only time should make us old."
"Not bad," I told him, and would tell him still.

Club Q

I stand for quest, which is to say mission,
as in "our mission is to provide
a safe space for you to be yourself,"
which is to say "it is not always safe
for you to be yourself." For queen,
as in a six-four Cher, hosting
Wednesday-night karaoke, always
the first and last to sing. For quarters,
which is to say jukebox, eight ball,
cigarettes, home. Of course, I stand
for queer. Which is to say unique,
which is to say alone. I am queer
in a military town where cadets
count out football scores in pushups
and Blue Angels bar up the sky.
For quarantine. For questioning.
As in, how long have you known?
As in, would you like to dance?
As in a dance floor, empty
save for two men kissing. A patio,
fenced in. The warmth of a firepit,
the sweetness of his saliva
after three gin and tonics. For quick,
which is to say alive, which is to say
mortal. I am quick as a number
scrawled on a cocktail napkin
between pages of a One-Year Bible
on a nightstand, quiet as the fist-
sized cloud rising from the sea
after Elijah slaughters his 450th
prophet of Baal. For quench:
to satisfy and to extinguish. I stand
for rainbow, and I stand for rain.

Mega Man

I'm a machine, an alpha. I go with my gut,
meet any Goliath on his turf, cut
him down with a well-placed shot. I turn elec-
tricks, whatever color I like, my blood to ice.
I can cream any master, be the fire
in his eyes. I'm the man. I'm the bomb.

I learn his patterns, parry his bombs,
get all up in his face, all up in his guts.
If I keep him running, he can never fire.
I own him with my fists, my uppercut
robotically smooth. I'm black ice.
He spins out. I press select, select, select.

Once he's sufficiently electrocuted,
I steal his clothes. I love his green bomber
jacket, his vintage snowsuit, ice
blue. For special occasions, I wear his guts
like pajamas. It's destiny. We were cut
by the same die, forged in the same fire.

He teaches me to survive, to spark fire
and catch the next man's kindling. O, my elect-
oral officials, my rock-crushes-scissors-cut-
paper dolls—each one a blond bomb-
shell of a man I gut as an angler guts
the catch he hooks from a hole in the ice.

I take what I need: his chest of ice,
his scissor legs, his great balls of fire,
his superior arms. There are always more guts
to uncoil, more brains purely electronic
as mine. We're wired, like all good bombs,
with the need to explode, to undercut

Mega Man

anything within blast range. Deep cuts
scar our fuselage. Left to our own devices,
we will never be defused. We'll bomb
a nation. We'll always be on fire,
an unbeatable boss. If desire is electric,
may we shock. May we spill our guts.

The Human Situation

Wednesday

I wake with the same erection I had during liftoff.
Cabin pressure, recycled air, a rhythmic, uterine rush.
My carry-on's fat with Classics. My tray table buckles
under the *Metamorphoses*, page marked with boarding pass.
I've checked the *Republic* and stowed St. Augustine. I pray
for delayed landing and nurse a cran-apple cocktail.
The four-ounce plastic taster won't stop sweating.

Below, the stark geometry of America's midsection:
vast circular fields irrigated by a central pivot compass
and sliced into perfect sixths. Reddi-wip contrails.
Cauliflower cumulonimbi. Our shadow grazes the earth,
compartment by logical compartment, until it's swallowed
by a larger shadow. Minor turbulence. A man tears a slit
into his package of nuts and empties it into his mouth.

Thursday

My sister and her husband have just returned from Istanbul.
She's wearing a sequined hijab. His English is spotty.
The turkey, as always, is far too large. We pray over it.
Before dessert, my father produces a Porky Pig cookie jar
filled with legal pad scraps, a Bible verse handwritten on each.
We all draw our scrap, unfold it, read it aloud. Dad explains
what each one makes him thankful for. The little things.

Once the carcass fits into the refrigerator, we break out
Taboo, "the Game of Unspeakable Fun."
If I want my team to guess "sister," I cannot say "apostate."
If I want my team to guess "love," I cannot say "cock,"
"lube," "fabulous," "lavender," "roommate," or "buddy."
The parents look over the children's shoulders. Vice versa.
I hold the buzzer's pink button until I'm told to stop.

Sunday

All flights canceled. On the news, a meager death toll:
three for the whole blizzard, all at the same time,
a mother and two sons retrieving supplies. Black ice.
Five-foot drift. The heat left on full blast
in their silver Escape. As usual, carbon monoxide,
the children first. "California plates,"
the locals cluck and switch back to the game.

I've warmed up to my old room's tacked-up playbills,
the Mondrian imitation waffling over the headboard.
My professor has granted my request for an extension.
I remove a ceiling panel and browse my library: Freshmen,
Unzipped, a yellowing catalog (Abercrombie and Fitch).
Inside my senior yearbook, I'm told, *You're going
places! Have a great summer! Never forget who you are!*

Heart Smart

Spell my name in Alpha-Bits,
a crisp golden kissogram. Be
my riboflavin, exceed my RDA.
You're quick, you're special. I'm sick
of turning tricks, fed up with poppers
and k-holes. My heart can't bear
another shredding, another tiger
with a neckerchief fetish. Two can-
not play at that game, Sam, and
deep down I prefer the side of the box
to the back. I may be a smidge loopy,
a tad flaky, but I'm steering this ship
in a totally new direction. I'm charming,
if not lucky. Here is my life.
Check it out. Ring me up.

Stick to the Subject

I saw the subject at Alter Ego today
working on his arms. I like the subject's arms.
They're not too vascular, proportionate
to his modest runner's build.
The subject has a good head shape
and a silvering buzzcut, as do many
of the thirtysomething subjects I've been seeing lately.

The subject and I were at the Atlantic
for Eighties night. We orbited each other
until we finally collided during "Major Tom."
We looked into each other's eyes and smiled
as if we knew exactly what would happen next.
Then they played "Beat It." I went off
on a tangent's moped, then on the tangent,

who is bald but otherwise pleasantly hairy.
He's in massage school. *Quelle chance!*
He and the subject run together Sundays
through the Bed & Breakfast District,
past the live oaks and azalea bushes. I asked
if he and the subject had ever hooked up.
He dodged the question. I walked home.

I saw the subject again tonight at the Triangle
with an object he met on the internet.
They were standing near the fire exit,
the object whispering into the subject's ear,
the subject laughing. I went for a smoke
on the patio and considered the Spanish moss,
which is neither Spanish nor a moss.

We Are the World

Part of me wishes they weren't plasma screens,
the waiting room's Panasonic televisions
glowing with a king of pop's solid gold
funeral. Part of me would like rabbit ears,

glass bulging and gray, a loose vertical hold,
some reassurance that what's inside
the machine is nothing like what's inside me.
Part of me wants poverty for consistency's sake.

TVs and clocks: to drain away the time
and spit it back. When I hear my name,
I enter Booth Seven, swallow a thermometer,
and say what I need to say: two yeses, 28 nos.

The entry site on my right arm's still bruised,
so let's do the left today, thanks. We remove
to the Fiesta Deck, to row after row of chaises-longues
and IV-bag cocktails. Nothing's audible

over the motors' pulse, but I can still see
Brooke Shields tower over a dense rank of children
and sing her silent elegy into the microphone.
The machines take what they want and return the rest.

Ladies and gentlemen of the donor floor,
we are the world. We pump our fists
for four draw cycles. The essence of us drips
the color of dehydrated pee into a plastic jug.

Unhooked, we will sign for our twenty bucks
and jab the straw into our Kool-Aid juice sack.
We will suck it dry and stumble our way
out double doors into the double sun.

Gainesville Sestina

In my village, the people ride cowboys
and thereby save horses, as advised by their Indian-
manufactured silk-screen tees. Sex workers
dodge water balloons hurled by policemen,
which, even in Florida, is not cool. Hipster bikers
sport mutton chops and cutoff jeans—soldiers

against the tyranny of fossil fuel, soldiers
with tattooed calves even the deftest cowboy
couldn't lasso. Remember when riding a bike
was dorky, a bourgeois hobby? Now it's indie,
subversive, an eco-friendly fuck-tha-police,
an homage to some abstract working

class, perhaps, one that never had to work
for the University, that never soldiered
through lunch rush at Reitz Union or policed
coolers at Griffin Stadium, where Cowboys-
to-be plow through ranks of Seminole Indians.
The truly poor do not ride fixed-gear bikes,

double-fixed or flip-flop. If they do bike,
it's when their cars have stopped working,
engines rusted, victims of an eternal Indian
summer. But when the DJ mashes up Soulja
Boy and Toby Keith at the hip-hop/cowboy
disco; or when, outside, a policewoman

lets a tipsy sorority sister cop
a feel of her steed's nose; or when a biker
revs his hog for a Saran-wrapped drag queen—that, *kemosabe*,
is what we call progress. Ask the construction worker
installing tanning beds in the dorms. Ask the soldier
recruiting privates outside Chick-fil-A. Ask the Indian

Gainesville Sestina

physicist who explains she is thirty-five, and Indian,
but takes a pamphlet anyway. It's like the old GPD
saying goes: "For a scrap of colored ribbon, a soldier
will fight to his death." Someone, someday, might break the cycle,
but the PhD candidates are too busy working
through Baudrillard's meditations on the Marlboro cowboy.

And me? Why, I'm one-sixteenth Cherokee. My bike's
a police-auction ten-speed. I work construction.
[Insert soldier.] See? [Insert cowboy.]

Heaven's Gates, Hell's Flames

Beyond the faux-*shōji* partition, a dreadlocked mother
shields her face with a menu. "Smoked. Eel,"

her son insists. "I want. The smoked. *Eel.*"
She is steadfast: "*California roll*, Oliver—

we discussed this in the car." Pretending to admire
the tank of silicone jellyfish, I smile at the smiling

cartoon children, arms joined, ringing Oliver's
Montessori school t-shirt. On the patio, his mustachioed Pops

sings their baby daughter a Leonard Cohen lullaby,
the kind of secular music my father forbade

around the time he forbade Disney and Red Devil hot sauce.
When we went out, it was always to Giovanni's, the $5 pizza buffet

halfway home from church, a dark, garlicky place
whose grease-stained cordons corralled us single-file

toward steaming circles of food, which we devoured
as long as football lit the hulking television.

Here, I had my first sip of flat, metallic O'Doul's.
Here, my brother and I raced to eat the most slices

and stumbled away from the table to stand, quarterless,
before the Street Fighter II cabinet and watch crude

ethnic stereotypes beat the shit out of each other.
How destined we were for failure those Sunday afternoons,

reaching up the prize chute of the claw machine
for the spotlit pile of Power Rangers, blackening the knees

of our church pants on the burnt-orange tile, returning like dogs
for seconds of the oily pizza we loved, all we could eat.

The Weekend After

We spent Independence Day
in Santa Fe.
The hotel was OK.
We found room to be gay

at restaurants, over beers,
in Georgia O'Keefe's early years.
We found room for tears.
We saw a Pixar movie, two queers

sobbing in the dark. Thank God something let us.
The week before, we'd learned your status.
And mine. It didn't get us
both. We were no longer lovers

in the carnal sense. We shared a queen
and left no stain.
The fireworks were canceled by the rain.
You complained

about my music, my driving, my silence.
I didn't argue, my feelings' absence
itself a kind of violence.
We took pictures in the ruins

of the Bandelier. We saw a stag.
We ate Frito pie out of the bag.
Climbing a ladder leaned against a crag,
you posed, one hairy leg

kicked up, fist under your beard.
We found room to be weird.
We idled on the shoulder till a storm cleared.
The end was closer than it appeared.

Arcade-Scented Candle

Heaven is a chorus boy. He twirls into the splits. He does not love you. You have some sense your life is working toward him; if you are very good, you might just get him for Christmas. He is a pony with beautiful haunches. He does not love you. If he had a smell, he would smell like blueberry muffins on a Saturday morning. But he has no smell. You do. You smell like an arcade, like burnt popcorn and spilled soda, like metal and ozone and decades-old nicotine. You are windowless yet full of light, every beep and whistle an invitation, every invitation outfitted with a slot for tokens. You are cheap. He is bathed in sunlight, shopping bags in each hand, stomping shirtless down the hallways of the mall in purple-tinted sunglasses and tight white jeans. He stomps right by you. At any moment he may break into song, fling the bags from his hands and open his arms as if for an embrace. You will never be in that embrace. If you could hold him, you would worry him in your palm like the malachite orb on your dresser. You would peer into his holes and marvel at his glittering imperfections. But he has no holes, he will not admit you. He doesn't even know what malachite is.

The Hobbyist

My father has taken to photographing flowers.
Wherever he travels, he looks up

the addresses of botanical gardens,
slings the strap of the big black Nikon

he's owned since my childhood
around his neck, and tilts the lens

into a poppy's crimson belly,
the ruffled folds of an iris's mouth.

His favorite shot is a closeup
of a bumblebee in the tawny center

of a sunflower. The frame is so tight,
you can see the insect's bristled tongue

siphoning nectar from the spiral.
For fifteen years, my father has worked

for a government weapons supplier.
He and my stepmother go to a church

where the pastor touches their foreheads
and they fall to the ground.

When he retires, they will move south,
where less care is needed for growth,

where the land and sea are not so far removed,
where, sixty years ago, my father was born.

He will find a new church, take more pictures,
visit his mother's grave. He will plant a garden,

The Hobbyist

with tulips, like the ones he saw in Amsterdam,
what he imagines heaven will look like.

Queries

Aa

"rough, cindery lava"
– *The Official SCRABBLE Players Dictionary*

As opposed to *pahoehoe*,
which advances in toes,
aa bulldozes the slopes,
leveling forests, swallowing villages
in yards-long balls
of basaltic dough.

Spines of clinker cascade
down its face into its gastric core,
a viscous hell that cools
into menhirs and obelisks jagging
through the saline air
of the archipelago.

It glows on the radar
of the *Magellan* probe
in white, meandering channels,
as opposed to *pahoehoe*,
whose tar is far hotter
but not half as reflective.

What does it matter,
this volcanist jargon,
the easiest palindrome
for cataclysm? Who needs it
outside of Scrabble, or maybe
some corner of Java,

Iceland, or Tierra del Fuego?
In a word, it adds up
to a spondee, disyllabic
like the babbling of infants,
or America
with the middle part blacked out.

Ab

"an abdominal muscle"
– *The Official SCRABBLE Players Dictionary*

Just one—the upper left, why not,
indented there like the first
cookie cut into the sheet of dough—
to show off in becomingly posed glossies.

Picture him in profile, reclining poolside,
his lower gut hidden under *Ulysses*,
his one dense knot
glistening with Coppertone.

Picture him in *Vogue Hommes*
modeling his chum Giorgio's white silk chemise
with its single cutout
you know where.

Up yours, ex-lover! Up yours, ennui!
He exudes core power,
very specific core power,
you don't know what you're missing,

do you? Who doesn't? Touch his tummy
right there, yes, there,
lick his little nested egg,
ignore the rest, it's none of your concern,

the ho-hum chest, the wispy fur ringing the nipples,
the good old penis. He didn't suffer
this long for you not to
touch him where it counts.

Al

"an East Indian tree"
— *The Official SCRABBLE Players Dictionary*

       To be the bearer   of   the vomit fruit
aka the famine fruit   the noni   the dog dumpling
your each massive offspring   a wart   with brown eyes
      spaced apart   just irregularly   enough
to induce   trypophobia   that primordial fear
      of porosity   the flesh beneath the pores
pyoid   thready   its flavor a mélange   of
      feta   jalapeño   &   yes   vomit
bilious & perversely   sweet   so foul
      as to be medicinal   some even say a
panacea   analgesic   aphrodisiac   anti-
inflammatory   bane of cancer AIDS & lice
      must be unbearable   wouldn't you say   al?
Yet your story is bigger   than your dumplings
      Your bark   makes batik   your leaves
delicious   cooked with coconut milk
      also make excellent nests   for ants

An

"indefinite article—used before words beginning with a vowel sound"
– *The Official SCRABBLE Players Dictionary*

a cento

An abomination
An uncle or a cousin or any blood relative
An emission of semen   an emission of semen   an emission of semen
An aroma pleasing to the LORD

An Israelite   an Egyptian
An act of impurity
An unclean place outside the town
An unclean animal   an animal found dead

An animal whose testicles are bruised
An animal from which a food offering may be made
An offering with thick loaves   an offering of the first fruits
An oven   an uncle   an offering of fire

An ordination   an oblation   an oath
An atonement for him   for them   for thyself
An inheritance for your children after you
An abomination   it shall not be eaten

Ar

"the letter R"
– *The Official SCRABBLE Players Dictionary*

Comparatively speaking, you're a real go-getter,
the one that makes the one that does a doer
or a good a better, a terminal creator,
an ace flying over and under the radar.
You regurgitate butter into rebutter.
The ridge of your brow climbs two times higher
when starting a sentence, then sinks a bit lower
the longer you ramble. You make quite the lover
with your tricks of the tongue, your oral manœuvres.
You're sour and bitter, a taste best acquired
through overindulgence, through left- and hangovers.
Your protean music changes keys across borders,
your guttural *schwesteren,* uvular *confrères,*
trilling *fratelli,* alveolar *kardeşler.*
Something about you is part of our nature,
our anger, our shivers, our begging to differ,
our names below "Yours," at the end of a letter.

As

"to the same degree"
– *The Official SCRABBLE Players Dictionary*

A as in app. B as in Medbh. C as in cnidoblast. D as in Medbh.
E as in eft. F as in effed. G as in effing. H as in aitch.
I as in N. J as in injuns. K as in Kombat. L as in Lladro.
M as in hmm. N as in Ng. O as in œuvre. P as in pfft.
Q as in -qatsi. R as in Dvořák. S as in a$$et$. T as in tchotchkes.
U as in onion. V as in *doble v*. W as in ewe.
X as in Xiu Xiu. Y as in ay ay ay. Z as in as if, as in as is.

—for Paul Muldoon

Ax

> "to work on with an ax (a type of cutting tool)"
> – *The Official SCRABBLE Players Dictionary*

I prefer this spelling, one woody vowel
hewn by the X, its blunt power
and implied danger, its cluster of noise
a strangled kiss—*kss, kss, kss*—
left at the end like a wound, a hickey
on a teenaged neck, though it's easy
to see the *e* anyway, bleeding through
in invisible ink, spectral as an echo
is the ghost of sound, as a tree might leave
in the earless forest, chopped down
by the ax of lightning, of beetle or beaver,
of age and rot, which ax us all the same
questions: what sound do you make when you're felled,
and how is it spelled?

Ba

"the eternal soul, in Egyptian mythology"
– *The Official SCRABBLE Players Dictionary*

I bang and my ba bangs.
When my ba bangs the men who dwell on Fire Island,
I bang the goddesses.

I am come, shining and ba-full, having swallowed all their magic.
I penetrate heaven
and tickle the egg that created me.

My ba won't be smoked out by the falcons.
My ba won't be hassled by the pigs.
My ba will pass by them in silence.

I have created my ba around me to teach it what I knew.
For my corpse's sake, my ba will not burn,
will not be held up by Osiris's thugs.

My heart is in my body; my corpse is in the earth.
I'm not crying about it.
I won't be kept from drinking water from the stream.

Bi

"a bisexual"
– *The Official SCRABBLE Players Dictionary*

I've known bisexuals. I've not known bis,
not one switch-hitter who identifies

as this adjective's nominalization.
One can *be* bi without much hesitation.

To be *a* bi is rather hard to swallow,
though logically it would seem to follow

a homo and a hetero, the latter
somewhat ungainly, and a little sadder;

but isn't all of it sort of sad, when spoken?
A gay. A straight. It's as if sex were broken

into pieces and we want words to fix it,
a bi made bi by say-so, *ipse dixit*,

a man in the Garden blindly sticking names
to all the reindeer and their reindeer games.

El

"the letter L"
– *The Official SCRABBLE Players Dictionary*

Jadedly twelfth, long tall El glowers leftwards.
Familiar lineup: triplet vowels,
paternal plosives, avuncular velars,
eleven motley lusterless losers.

El gallops like hell, trampling far-flung fields,
fallow & fertile. Stallion & filly, literal & metaphorical—
el rules all
duplex classifications silly. El

reflects, realizing *le*. Elle
materializes, allowing themself
likeness. Loveliness. Believe yourself
always, pellucid soliloquist, lapidary beanpole, middle child.

Em

"the letter M"
– *The Official SCRABBLE Players Dictionary*

Ohio boundary? My woe!
You adore—booty—no?
The shape of nature, sir!
Dovetail! Truly tented—donkey show!

Embowered—boy toy—hoards!
A whirlpool fuck—I beg—
Lonesome talent—love thine jungle—
Mining taboo drag.

Ex

"to cross out"
– *The Official SCRABBLE Players Dictionary*

X went to a different ~~vocational~~ high school
and misspelled ~~lovebola~~ lovable on a valentine.
X^2 had ~~halitosis~~ a ~~tiny~~ car and wrote ~~affected~~ queer
love poetry full of words like "staid." X^3 was
a ~~techie~~ theater major with a concentration in sound
who snuck me backstage and ~~dry rubbed against~~ kissed me
on a ~~sawdust-covered~~ set piece while the speakers played
~~Backstreet Boys~~ Massive Attack. X^4
visited from ~~Texas A&M~~ Rice ~~once~~
a few weekends to ~~blow~~ play me in Scrabble
~~in the closet while my roommate slept.~~
I ~~vomited California roll nori after ten shots~~
~~of peppermint Schnapps~~ partied at X^5's loft
~~and left my socks in his toilet~~, where I
met X^6—not the X^6 who ~~snorted~~
~~crystal meth off my Victorian lit anthology~~
went to my college—the X^6 who flew
me out to Walla Walla to meet his feminist
commune and picnic and play Boggle
late into the night, the X^6 with whom
I talk mad shit about X^5 to this day.
I don't remember X^7's name, but I do
remember ~~taking mushrooms and~~ watching
Full Metal Jacket and blowing smoke
out his blinds ~~and never being able to get it up~~.
And X^8, sweet, smart X^8, whom I remember
~~less and less~~ every time I hear ~~"Psycho Killer"~~
Talking Heads, how we sang "Life ~~During~~
~~Wartime~~" at karaoke, how ~~I~~ we broke
up ~~with him~~ at a ~~White Trash~~ party ~~in a Speedo~~
~~after I confessed to having cheated on him~~
~~with three other guys~~ while someone's iPod
played "Crosseyed ~~and Painless~~"—X^8, I promise
you are ~~not~~ the last man I'll reduce to ~~tears~~ song.

42

Ha

"a sound of surprise"
– *The Official SCRABBLE Players Dictionary*

Half holier-than-thou hallelu-yahoo, half Halliburton-championing have-over-have-notter. Happened—through the stealthy mechanisms the self-loathing have, chatrooms & whatnot—upon a shady Lothario-for-hire. Fashioned a handle, Thaddeus Haggerty, that haunted Hampton Inns. Alcohol, halitosis, prophylactics, hair. Methamphetamines. Whole-hearted thank-yous. Washed his hands. Gnashed his teeth. Hallucinated. Hankered. Snatched his parish's cash & bequeathed it to his pusher-man, who eventually Deep-Throated him. Hatched alibis. Hightailed to Heroica Nogales. *Hasta la vista.*

Id

"a part of the psyche"
– *The Official SCRABBLE Players Dictionary*

My id is the assistant manager
of my psychic thrift store,
scowling at his guests,
the kids most of all, swallowing
chess pawns and flushing
the bowls of the men's room
for sport. He hates men,
their big dumb chests and faces
creased and chiseled by charm.
He takes long, lonely smoke breaks
in the throes of Halloween peak hours,
horks phlegm through the chilled air,
and wedges the fire door open
with a knockoff Ugg (an Ugh)
to let the trails of his Kools
snake into the changing rooms.
His heart is a rack of sweaters
too dense to slide the hooks.
He dreams of going on a cleanse:
no more smokes, no more cold-brew,
the drugs he takes to sleep, to wake,
to hope—everything must go.
He dreams of being a nightmare
crashing through cemetery gates,
cardboard gravestones crumpling
beneath his authentic hooves.

Is

> "It depends on what the meaning of the word 'is' is."
> – William Jefferson Clinton

How fondly I remember the last impeachment,
how much care was taken for the children.
Linda Ellerbee, on a special edition of *Nick News*,
explaining what fellatio meant
to a circle of fifth graders,
spoke gingerly as a school nurse, a practiced kind
of nurturing. I felt a proud exemption.
I'd given up Nickelodeon for MTV.
The stained dress, the cigar, John Goodman
in drag as Linda Tripp, each minutia
of the great, national foofaraw
confirmed what I already knew:
I would never find the right woman.

A church favorite: God always answers,
but not always *yes*. In the waning Clinton days,
the sight of any shirtless man
sent me straight to my bedroom,
to the sheets my mother dutifully,
unquestioningly, washed. And on the news,
night after night, the president's latest sound bite
made it seem as if "is"
could have meant anything at all,
protean as snow. I had yet to learn
the third person, but I knew the present
meant a pleasure so filled with dread
it threatened to swallow the future.

Twenty years later, the closing statements
of the latest impeachment hearings
melt in with a late November flurry.
The airplane carrying a man I love
has just let go of the tarmac.
There is nothing inappropriate between us.

Is

Alone with the TV, the whirr of a furnace,
and the dregs of the coffee he brewed,
I wonder what the children I don't have
will remember of their first season
of scandal, what words, familiar, innocuous,
have already started sprouting hairs.

Om

"a mantra used in contemplation of ultimate reality"
– *The Official SCRABBLE Players Dictionary*

Have you been home the past four years?
Is this where you clipped your fingernails,

listened to the traffic, and hung three self-
portraits on the gallery wall?

The little cross-stitch of the moonlit squirrel,
the taxidermied tarantula—

what do these bring if not joy?
Try hard enough and you'll say something

you'll remember later, like what you heard on the radio,
from a writer: *Better done than good.* Suffer

the pain of the next word, the beautiful turn
into a dead end: the mere fact of Snapchat.

Remember the man in the hot-yoga studio, naked except
for the black spandex censor's bar over his pelvis.

Remember how you rubbernecked
to watch his downward dog. *Husband*

your gaze, you remembered from the radio,
but heard *husband your gays*

always, a different breed of mindfulness, mirrors
on every wall, so much sweat in your towel

you could wring it out into the sink.
It's time to stop smoking, to call the hotline.

Om

Don't you want to work on yourself
with all its crumpled notes? even if

it means giving away your secrets,
like the nose hairs you must trim tonight

or you'll be doomed to a life of competitive Scrabble
and meaningless sex, meaning less sex

and more work, more play-
mates, fewer soulmates. You know better

than to feed the listing tic, but
you are in love with turns, with change,

summer to autumn, when the fruit is fat
and darkness raises its voice. By the way,

it's a show. There are literally thousands
of people watching, hopefully drinking

the Cran-Raspberry La Croix you are so happy
to be sipping this cool October night

as the bass from Lincoln rattles your apartment
windows and you remember to breathe.

Qi

"the vital force that in Chinese thought is inherent in all things"
– *The Official SCRABBLE Players Dictionary*

Qi hides in ninja dipstick, bunkbed weft, oba tuba, haruspex heme, the many, the few, the wandering Jew. Oy! It can cloy.

Qi of basilisk is qi of dipteron. Qi of zed is qi of ex. Qis ovulate hymns. Qis hog areolas. Qis smite fags.

I spotted my qi in the cays, having sex with vogie gogo boys. Stoical, loftier-than-thou, I was all like, umm, pfft.

Who valuates qi? Ha! Blindest dunce, lamest oaf, dreaming pet civets. Qi adores fetor, purges fivers. Qi nixes ingots and narghiles. Qi raises hob.

For starters, qi joins logic to shrubs. Qi is on the dole and the pol. Qi is a pinup fined for excessive feting, an ogre doused in *eau de prawn*. Qi awes and joys, an obedient ox, an erne's vim, a qat cigar. It mucked out and lucked about. I'm a fan.

Qi is a vibe. Qi makes a thing radiant and clean shaven. Qi can be worn in lieu of a tux. Qi makes a pillow pillowy. It exerts henrys, wins queridas, and defogs all that is true.

Qi is a con envisaged by intoners and feigners, their maws lusting after your loins. It relegates mobility to toil. Be advised, you will be larruped. You will be gulfed.

Qi is peace. Qi is jnana. Qi is podcast, bongo, bongo. Is qi me? Naw, qi is aye. Qi is fiz, qi is is. Oh, qi, ye is awl.

Ta

"an expression of gratitude"
– The Official SCRABBLE Players Dictionary

Ta, Mom,
>for the word *ducky*
>for the Nintendo
>for the criminality of insulting Mickey Mouse in the state of Florida
>for McDonald's failed $20 burger, "The Ron Supreme"
>for the Super Nintendo
>for bailing Mike and me out of the Royal Rangers
>for bailing Max and Jack out of the pound, two times each
>for paying me $5 to watch *The Wizard of Oz*, which of course I loved
>for the Nintendo 64
>for leaving spaghetti and sauce on the stove after dress rehearsals
>for letting me come out when I was ready
>for the $200 in credit card charges I made at Diesel, which you
>>thought was an auto shop
>
>for the Saturn, which still runs
>for taking the call
>for the pills
>for the Wii
>for us

Ta, Mike,
>for making amends
>>for not protecting me
>>for calling me your little sister
>>for squirting Fruitopia in my face at the bus stop
>>for mocking me when I was too resigned to wipe the syrup off
>>>my glasses
>>
>>for tilting my just-finished 1,000-piece U.S. Presidents jigsaw
>>>puzzle off the card table and laughing when I cried
>>
>>for your cruel, sexy jock friends who played skins-and-skins
>>>two-on-two on our driveway and bullied me mercilessly
>>>and confused the fuck out of my pubescent brain, driving
>>>me to punch through my bedroom window screen,
>>>among other fits of homoerotic pique

>   for pushing me down the stairs
> for protecting me

Ta, Scott Major,
> for being my only friend for a solid three years and auditioning with me for the Spring play, "Occupation: Murder," with an actual monologue about the word "ta," the details of which I've otherwise forgotten

Ta, Mrs. Bos & Mrs. Kop,
> for living up to your names

Ta, Mr. Kool,
> for not living up to yours

Ta, Mrs. Loomis,
> for telling me, a high-school sophomore, I was "definitely smarter" than you
> for writing "beautiful" on my terrible poem about *The Good Earth*, which I still have not read
> for giving me 110% on our African-diaspora oral examination, a format I proposed
> for indulging my voracious Leo appetite for praise
> for Liking my humble-brag Facebook posts
> for the gift of favoritism, damn the expense

Ta, James,
> for Italo Disco and the Best of Bollywood Volume One, Pet Shop Boys and "Menergy," crime jazz and car rock, Charlotte Gainsbourg, Beirut, Stephen Merritt, Peter Bjorn & John
> for microcinema, Jan Terri, Ryan Trecartin, the Aurora Picture Show, Wes Anderson, and Preston Sturges
> for "the ol' sushi strainer," the first full beard I ever kissed
> for "Dr. House and Dr. Bones"
> for the Art Car Parade
> for letting me cat-sit Gertrude & Claudius

Ta

    for the phrase *flea dust*
    for steeping me in the Bayou City while I had the chance
    for making me feel wise beyond my years when the opposite was the case
    for accepting my apologies
    for seeing me off

Ta, the state of Florida.

Ta, Pensacola,
    for your heraldry
Ta, St. Augustine,
    for the word *globster*
Ta, Gainesville,
    for the treehouse
    for Bubbles
    for Dude
    for no central heat
    for the dance of the Smathers Library shelves
    for *Scorpio Rising* and *Taxi Driver*
    for "Who cooks for you?"
    for actual piles of alligators
    for alligator chili
    for black-bean quinoa
    for salsa cereal
    for Hare Krishna salad dressing
    for Newports and Presidente
    for treating my pleurisy
    for the word *pleurisy*
    for the word *bittern*
    for the student whose evaluation insisted I "not take everything so personal"
    for my poem, "Personal"
    for my poem, "Teaching a Gay Poem"
    for pre-*Drag Race* Jade Jolie
    for my cohort

Ta

for the trellis
for doubt
for all the bigger fish

Ta, my depression,
    for the days off work
    for teaching me to appreciate k.d. lang
    for slowing my roll, as the kids say
    for disinterring my live-buried childhood, brushing the soil off its
        body, pumping air in its lungs, and making it speak the terrible
        things it had been led to believe:
            love never lasts
            not even the other faggots want you
            you have been left for dead
    for leaving me at a loss for words
    for needing more than words
    for needing sobs and wails, screams into throw pillows, bawling and
        puling, snot, silent tears in grocery aisles, on the phone, the
        Free Mall Ride, therapists' couches and yoga mats and gay-
        church pews, crying until my throat was sore, crying until my
        tear ducts bubbled
    for not being *about* anything
    for raising your voice loud enough for me to acknowledge you
    for shutting the fuck up

Ta, Dad,
    for your pronouncements of love
    for your polite articulation of how you believe I am keeping myself
        from happiness
    for your contempt for victimhood—my whetting stone
    for living through a broken heart
    for never exactly leaving
    for scanning the photographs
    for teaching me to read
    for teaching me to use chopsticks
    for telling me to stop you

for your admittedly terrible Christmas and birthday presents
for your underlying mildness
for saying you're proud   (I believe you)
for making me believe and not believe in God

Ta, God,
   for existing and not existing
   for being non-binary that way: real and fake, a quantum
   for being cooler than religion
   for being way cooler than church
   for the baroque art of blasphemy
   for the Bhagavad Gita
   for the Tao Te Ching
   for the Bible, its many horrors and absurdities and ditties and arcana
   for *Paradise Lost*
   for Leibnitz
   for Nietzsche
   for Flannery O'Connor
   for, believe it or not, *Game of Thrones*
   for the beauty of men
      their unmown stomachs and legs
      their thick, bosky eyebrows
      their stupid pouts and exaggerated repose
      their cubist chests and cocks and posteriors
   for the words *cum gutters*
   for the word *callipygian*
   for the sound of tangerine wedges as they separate

Ta, Scrabble,
   for the words—the glorious, copious words
   for OXO, FREMD, ANESTRI, and ROLAMITE
   for BERIBERI, GRIGRI, JUJU and DIKDIK
   for "The POO List"
      for FAGGIER, FAGGOTIER, NANCIER, and QUEENIER
      for SHITBAG and SHITLOAD and CHICKENSHITS
      for FUCKUPS and FUCKWITS and FUCKOFFS

Ta

for front hooks: (x)YLEM, (f)AIRWAY, (w)AGELESS, (o)CHERISH
for end hooks: BAZOO(m), BELIE(f), FIXIT(y)
for miniaturizing achievement
for the word *Gibsonization*
for your uneasy but not irreconcilable relationship to poetry
for the unprofitability of both
for SPONDAIC and CAESURAE, SESTINA and GHAZAL
for POETESS and POETLIKE and POETLESS
for the delicacy of an endgame setup being not unlike the
    composure of a sonnet
for anagrams being not unlike rhyme
    for MASTERS / STREAMS
    for DEFIANT / FAINTED
    for GYRATED / TRAGEDY
for phonies, challenged and unchallenged
for the hadal depths of mastery
for everlasting love
for word fetishists,
    may we never be cured.

Us

"the objective case of the pronoun we"
— *The Official SCRABBLE Players Dictionary*

Yet we remember the curve, what we felt of grace
before we learned   what grace meant,
before divorce   ate childhood,
a body in   perpetual   emotion.
There can't   be a we   anymore.
Only when we   lived together, a family
of four, game night   every Friday, dice
or a card deck or a blank   tile on a rack.
Forget   who won—we all   played
together   on blue Formica,   the tank
of life   bubbling above   the knife
drawer, one   thin line   dividing
the golden flank   right through
the eye to the tailfin.   Naturally, we
knew they would float   to the top one day,
yet we remember the figure, their dance: captivity.

Za

"a pizza"
– *The Official SCRABBLE Players Dictionary*

Zeugma, that hungry trope: *he sliced the pizza*
and his heart in perfect twenty-sixths. The poor verb,
bloated with the literal and metaphoric,
collapses, overfed,
drowsy with figuration and extra cheese.
Eat up. If ever there were an American motif—
food for thought and the occasional gag—
gluttony would fit the bill. We sandwich
hamburgers between donuts. We honor pi
in March with lemon meringue. We go on hajj,
journeying across state lines to Shake Shack,
Kansas City barbecue pits, the first Taco Bell,
lifted from its foundation and into Elysium,
more or less. We have a national religion:
not Christianity, nor humanism, nor atheism, but Sbarro,
Orange Julius, Little Caesar's. The Styrofoam cup
perched on the counter at DQ
questions our mettle: *Tips are NEVER*
Required but ALWAYS
SUPER APPRECIATED. We have every right
to order around our servers and off the menu
unless decency intercedes. In which case, mazel tov!
Virtue is a dance we all know
well enough: to leave the last slice in the box,
x'es scored through the cardboard, until somebody
younger and hungrier ruins the waltz.

Quotidian

State of the Union

—after Jericho Brown

I knew I was out of shape by week four of the shutdown.
The Senate floor was strewn with dusty dumbbells. The House was

my house. That year, before breakfast, lunch, and dinner, I prayed
the president would go to prison. Then, the president went

to McDonald's. His doctors claimed he weighed slightly less than a thousand
quarter-pounders. What is the professional term for a man who lies

for his boss? I asked my personal trainer. He told me, a Personal Trainer.
Then, he said, "Let's bang out some supermans." Then, he said, "Good job."

I always trust a man in Under Armor. My reward: whey protein isolate,
whey protein concentrate, whey peptides, soy lecithin, sucralose, salt.

No one in America is healthy. It's all my fault. Three to four times a week,
another life is ruined by smoke or sugar or, sure, why not, my guns.

American Gothic

The farmer is in love with his work,
not with you, who are not his wife
but his daughter, plain as the pitchfork

clutched in his hand, white as the briefs
around his loins. Some poison
keeps the men away. A thief

stole Lindy's baby. Soon enough, Japan
will plant its flag in European soil.
You close your eyes and see *La Marianne*

bare-chested on a battlefield of oiled,
Gallic bodies, tramping as if through lanes
of *Zea mays*. Change is cruel.

Not long ago, you ate your first sardine.
Bathed in oil, shipped from Nantucket
to Des Moines, it slid, pristine,

headfirst, down your throat. You didn't like it.
The taste stuck to your mouth like tallow
to a frying pan. In the shallow bucket

of your stomach, you felt a crow's
feet gently begin to kick, a little jerk
keeping time with your heart's adagio.

Unmentionables

"We greet your defect with seriousness and responsibility."
    —*from* Nonverbal Communication,
        Jurgen Ruesch and Weldon Kees

Control lingerie.
Truss, garter, girdle.
Staid references,

staider referents.
A storefront vitrine:
shapewear on headless

busts, compression socks
squashing spider veins
into bloodless legs.

Off-white torsos, half-
mummified in twelve-
inch reinforced Zip-

-n-Trim waistbands, posed
against the shadows
of the hernial,

the scoliotic,
the edematous,
the gouty, the chafed.

"Expertly Fitted,
Made to Order": vows
in thin script, a tail

curling off the M,
a dainty brace from
Fitted to *Order*.

To the Observant Motorist Who Called Me Faggot

We have names for things we barely understand.
The Doppler Effect, for instance. You have no idea

how it works, and neither do I, but I'm sure we both
can appreciate the way it splits

a word in two clean syllables:
the fag from it, the it from fag.

I like to think of myself as a hyphen.
To you, maybe, I'm a piñata:

gaily colored, filled with sugar,
battered open by blindfolded children.

Maybe, in your life's game of Tag,
I am, perpetually, It. Or

maybe, after all, I am nothing, something
approached, named, and sublimated.

I've thought of several names for you. "Chuck"
seemed appropriate. But without a name, you are

your Civic, its rattling speakers, its red taillights
forever headed south.

Bingo

It's true: I lived next to a bingo hall
much of my life unawares. Maybe you too
have felt the itch: out of the blue,
you hang a left at the Korean Presbyterian Church
you've breezed right by for years, and holy hell,

there it is, some dull place risen to arch
significance by virtue of your never having seen it.
It's clear you can't live another minute
without going inside. I did. I haven't left
for fifteen years. A neutered voice still calls,

"B 4. 4 under the B." The white balls
boil in their plate-glass cauldron till they're sucked
up a tube and spit down a spiraling shaft.
The flashboard lights each number as it's picked.
There is no skill required but obsession.

It's not that bad. There are concessions:
plastic ramekins filled to the shallow brim
with hot Crayola cheese, served with clips
of pristinely round GM tortilla chips,
soft serve, Hot Tamales, Diet Coke.

The hall has maybe half the warmth of home:
a place to sit, an oft repeated joke—
"The tumor was benign. B 9 ... O 60,
O 60, Grandma's getting frisky"—
the mollifying artifice of rhyme.

Yet scratch this gentle humor and you'll sniff
the stench of death. We run from a cliff
whose edge runs after us. The fall grows nearer
with every cheerful number. A matter of time,
and it comes to pass: you are a hearer,

Bingo

not a sayer of the bingo. Luck's razor
slices through the air. You're a loser.
Or you will be next round, I promise.
The frisky grandma will turn cold, indignant.
The tumor will recur, this time malignant.

And you'll go on. You'll tear off the spent sheet
and hope next round's the one that makes you famous.
You'll clutch your lucky dauber. You'll compete,
remembering the advantages you've earned,
the reflexes you've honed, the money you've burned.

Of all the years I've lived here, I've won twice.
The first time, just nineteen, I earned a grand
on a progressive blackout. I couldn't understand
how wealthy I'd become. My net worth doubled.
"Congrats," I heard, in Minnesota Nice.

The second was a decade later. Stubbled,
fingers stained with ink and nicotine,
I was a regular, a bitter queen
upon a folding throne, my screw-top scepter
the one and only wand I'd ever held.

I'd almost forgotten how the game was spelled,
the letters disappearing one by one.
I was a dog who didn't have a farmer
or a name. My money was almost gone.
And then they called O 60, the upper-right

corner to complete my Krazy Kite.
I had to split the hundred-dollar purse
with a septuagenarian majorette,
but half a prize can pay off all the debt
you owe to luck. Now I am the devil

Bingo

in a sequined tux. I broke the curse
and doled out all the pieces to my rivals:
a chunk to the lady in the fuchsia Rascal scooter,
a shard to everyone with a pricy computer
that dabs the numbers for them. Seems like cheating,

but those whose buy-ins are the highest
are never guaranteed the win. The parvenu beating
the veteran, the wheel of fortune biased
toward the yutz with one pathetic card—
it keeps me guessing, the sweetest reward.

And from this desperate place I write this poem
in turquoise dauber ink. And from this game
I make myself a solitary home.

gay4pay

our foreskin
is ur skin

click <u>here</u> to
learn more skin

watch straight dudes
hardcore skin

they need it
their poor skin

cum on GERMS!
restore skin

Teaching a Gay Poem

You'll see—the air conditioning
in your classroom will malfunction
in protest. The pollen-dusted windows
will not open no matter how hard you thrust
your palms against their lower sashes.
A bottom-line-minded ombudsman had them soldered
shut to keep the pigeons out (long
before the Information Age, as we've come to call it).
These days, if you somehow manage to sneak a pigeon
into an Introduction to Poetry class,
the students will not have the wherewithal
to describe it. They will begin to ask
about the person who made the pigeon,
if this individual is a pigeon him/herself
and, if so, whether s/he writes poems for that reason.
You'll refer to the syllabus, how it does not say
"Freshman/Sophomore *Ornithology*" at the top
of Page One in centered 14-point Garamond,
but by now their line of inquiry will have turned
to you—your sweat, your shirt-sleeves rolled up
past your biceps, your armpit-hairs peeking out
their vermicular heads. What kind of sick
show-and-tell is this? they'll wonder.
And as you stammer on about identity,
the pigeon will lift silently off your desk
and batter its filthy, feathered body against the glass.

Dating My Mom

My mom looks nothing like her profile picture.
Untied, her hair is a wimple
dyed Clairol Nutmeg.

Her bangs brush the top of her glasses.
Their Transitions lenses waffle
in the Macaroni Grill's chiaroscuro lighting.

Her rosacea blooms. For the occasion,
she has dressed in a blouse
printed with dandelion clocks.

I ask my mom the usual questions.
She has two brothers, a pharmacist
and a prison guard. She is a dog person.

She goes on about her ex-husband,
her "low bullshit tolerance." Her birthday
is exactly one week after mine.

A list of things my mom hasn't heard of:
micro-cinema, bubble tea, Chechnya,
Whoopi Goldberg, fractals.

When I return from the restroom,
my mom is zipping
the rest of the bread into her purse.

I drive my mom home. She asks me in.
A spaniel braces against her windowsill,
baying. I feign an allergy.

She tilts my head forward and kisses
the whorl on the back of my scalp—
a benediction, an apology.

White Chickens

Yeah right, replies so much. I depend upon myself, not your wheel, nor your polite chickens.
My love got lost at the Mineral Show and fell in with a flock of malachite chickens.

Even my grandmother has an iPhone. She texts rarely, hunting for the emoji *juste*.
Her daughter moved to a red state, bought a twelve-gauge, shoots coyotes who try to bite chickens.

So much depends upon history or, more broadly, Social Studies. My high-school rain dance
conjured only a happenstance of glitter and rare, collectible Rainbow Brite chickens.

Everyone's crazy about protein these days. Every salad is a green meat-vehicle.
All these beautiful men at the gym strut like hypertrophied, hey-you-wanna-fight chickens.

Tonight's special is drenched in a demi-glace of esoterica and simple syrup.
Oh, hi. I'm James, but you can call me So Much. See you at the White Party. Invite chickens.

Lemmings

"All Beautiful the March of Days,"
        my research tells me, was the hymn
a British sound programmer chose
        to mash up with a Morricone theme
            and score the game

I played all day when I was seven,
        herding sprites through a hundred hells
into a hundred off-screen heavens.
        A satisfaction came with every kill:
            an open well,

a gout of flame, a claw, two taps
        on X to make the countdown start
and nuke their species off the map.
        My father, the debugger, helped me cheat
            till I got smart.

Twenty years later, I pressed pause,
        sipped a gin martini, smoked,
and thought about the man I was.
        I rented a poet's house. I wrote in chalk
            on the sidewalk

and passed it off as concrete verse.
        I left erasure to the rain.
Inside: the edge of the universe,
        the lemmings dropping one by one. My brain
            said, *play again.*

Magnavox Opus

There are extinct arts,
one of them being
the way my grandfather built a library

of movies taped off television,
twelve hundred cassettes' worth
in generic, yellowing sleeves,

their labels faced out,
filled in his cramped hand—
[title (year) running time]—

and curated to his convenience—
all three *Star Wars* movies
on different tapes, pirated

from different channels—no regard
for genre—a Capra/Spielberg/
Kurosawa triple-feature—

whatever was on that week
according to the saddle-stitched,
finger-blackening listings

in the Sunday *Post-Dispatch*,
movies printed four cells wide
with sparing, one-line synopses—

"Hazing horror on sorority row,"
"Western"—
each recording punctuated

by the proof
of his watching:
the briefest glimpse

Magnavox Opus

of a Coke's fizzing brim
before the tape cuts out
and cuts back in

on a preview of what was once
the nightly news—then back to
Back to the Future—

and his catalog,
the red spiral notebook he kept
within arm's reach of his recliner

in the wood-paneled basement—
its graphed pages portioned out
in alphabetical sections, a little space

at the end of each for titles yet to air,
every entry with a number
corresponding to a labeled drawer

in one of a dozen cabinets
no longer manufactured
for a format no longer used,

carted out of his split-level home
with the tapes still inside—
leaving just the catalog

with its little list of lasts:
*The Last of the Mohicans, The Last
American Hero, The Last Man on Earth…*

Episode 60

"Ozymandias"

The camera lingers on the barren land.
We've been here before, this cradle of red stone,
blue sky. A blaze of bullets boils the sand.
Walt's brother's dead, his corpse a damning frown
buried where the cash was. On command,
Walt shakes the killer's hand. This can be read
poetically: all the evil things
our hero cooked to keep his family fed
have burned the kitchen down. The means appear
to justify the ends. We've watched like kings,
bingeing seasons whole, streaming despair,
observing the ways a person can decay.
The ending credits roll. Our minds are bare,
our spirits numb. We do not look away.

Self-Portrait as Articulated Wall

March 7, 2019

In the Denver Design District, I stand,
  my 33 years stacked on top of each other
    like Tinkertoys sprinkled with pigeon shit,
      black pores, pock marks, all the various flaws
        in my skin some hue between mustard and gold.
      I look on the new Starbucks where the model
    train store recently derailed, the Sam's Club
  parking lot recycling SUVs, a mother-to-be
nesting in the northernmost median. Is she
  the same goose as last year? I can still picture
    her goslings, five pollen-colored gutter babies
      stopping traffic, so smitten were the shoppers
        at the fuzz, the waddle of the freshly hatched.
      One woman tried to feed them wasabi peas.
    My father left Germany behind to raise me
  and, once I had been raised, disappeared.
The other children pointed at me, laughing
  from minivans on I-25, headed to Bible Camp
    from the heart of Colorado Springs. They still
      call me "French Fries." I've grown to accept it
        as a compliment. I am all American, democratic
      as a Burger King crown, flimsy, iconic, garish,
    quaint, forgettable, depending on the angle,
  the light, the weather. This late winter day,
as the snow melts off my shelves, I weep.
  Chinook winds blow drops onto the asphalt,
    onto your upturned face, my solitary admirer.
      Inviting at ground level, my winding concrete
        staircase climbs nine stories, a height vertiginous
      as the dignified cliffs to my west. To scale me
    is prohibited and practically irresistible.
  Do so at your own risk. I may be here
the rest of my life, the rest of yours.

Sincerely, Chipotle

I could talk about sincerity,
how men, for centuries, have dreamt it meant
without wax, inventing honey-mongers
barking "*Sine cera*!" in the Forum,
shifty sculptors patching flaws in marble,
just-so stories, sticky as the truth.

Or I could talk about the word chipotle,
Nahuatl name for smoked, dried jalapeño,
its t and l so tempting to transpose
that some believe Nick Nolte is its rhyme.
Maybe your dad pronounces it this way
despite your wincing, or because of it.

I shouldn't talk about your dad. Or me—
Millennial gringo in a cubicle,
partial to Zelda, yoga, and pipe dreams
buoyed by Zoloft and a master's degree
IKEA-framed in a Denver bachelor pad—
though I could talk about that at some length.

Let's talk about your last experience
at one of our 2,000-plus locations.
I'm sorry. Truly sorry. For the food,
not quite as good as you remembered it,
the rice too firm, the beans congealed, the steak
nine bucks and dry as Jack Link's jerky.

I'm sorry for our haste to make your tacos,
the look we gave you when you said, "Slow down!"
I mean to say *we're* sorry. And we mean it.
No matter the ten thousand times we've said it,
no matter the degree of the offense,
we find our sorrow. *Nous sommes désolés*.

Sincerely, Chipotle

Let's talk in French. Let's soufflé, sous-vide.
Let's julienne an onion, let's mise-en-place.
Our CEO's a chef, you may have heard.
Great guy, nice jeans, will chat you up at parties,
was great on Oprah all those years ago
before—I guess you'd call it, *le déluge*.

Let's not talk about E. coli. Sure,
you've heard of it, just as you must have heard
of Scientology or crystal meth,
a far-flung threat become a household name.
It seems alarmist. Then, your neighborhood
Chipotle is a vector of disease.

People talk. The internet, like water,
transmits the smell of blood in all directions.
At first, it's customers who bleed. Then us.
Once doting magazines ink exposés.
Shares nosedive. Executives resign.
The Christmas party's canceled. Lines are short,

and nobody complains. My cube-mates yack
on Slack, check Facebook, drink seasonal IPAs,
and never leave a minute late. I promise,
we are decent people. But it's nice,
for once, to only say, "I'm sorry, sir,"
thirty-seven times a day, at most.

Let us forget about the General Queue,
the ever-mounting heap of misspelled woes
typed with furious, shaky thumbs on phones
by strangers in restaurants ten states away.
Let the grill be cold, the fryer drained,
the guacamole sealed in plastic wrap.

Sincerely, Chipotle

Talk is cheap. Creative is a noun.
Our guests are always guests, not customers.
Don't say healthy. Don't say serious.
Don't say, "I'm sorry that you had raw chicken";
say, "Sorry to hear that. That sounds truly awful."
It's really not that bad, but there are days

when I can only talk about the end,
my sudden, bitter walk away from years
apologizing to the void, from work
done not for love but for sincerity,
the needy ghost of Real America
eating a steak burrito, just like me.

I'd like to talk about that day. For lunch,
I'll go to the arcade on Blake and 5th,
the one with beer on tap, and drink my way
through twenty quarters' worth of BurgerTime.
By five, I'll finally get to Level Four,
where Peter Pepper meets his pickled end.

We'll never talk again. I won't write back.
I'll bury you beneath the mound of books
I'll finally read. I'll write my hidden words.
I'll spend my savings down to triple digits,
wake late, sleep late, sink back into the life
I lived before I said, "Let's make this right."

I take it back, about sincerity.
I can't talk about it, not sincerely.
Its etymology, the real one, I forget—
something predictable as "not a lie."
Introverts are good at saying sorry,
little else. And even that's a stretch.

Sincerely, Chipotle

You want to talk to somebody who cares?
Such people are in short supply, I've found.
My mother, and most likely yours, are two.
Perhaps a teacher from many years ago,
the one who writes the grownup you and asks
if you still write, or doesn't ask, but wishes.

You want to talk to somebody who'll listen?
There might be more of those. Professionals,
mostly, myself excluded. Therapists,
who listen better and are better paid.
Public defenders. Hotline operators.
Masseurs. Financial planners. Prostitutes.

You want to talk? Then talk. *Well, OK. First,*
let me just start by saying, I love Chipotle.
I sometimes go two times a day, no joke.
The gals at my Chipotle know my order
by heart: a bowl (I'm celiac), brown rice,
black beans, no meat (I'm vegetarian)—

Uh huh. I'm here. I'm listening. Keep talking—
extra fajitas, a little bit of corn,
a lot of sour cream, and guac, of course.
I'm like a member of the family.
And I'm not someone who complains for fun.
I work in customer service, too, in fact,

and I could talk about entitlement,
folks who think the universe owes them…stuff,
who think "the customer is always right"
is meant to be taken literally. As if!
I'm not expecting anything for free.
I don't want coupons, anything like that.

Sincerely, Chipotle

*I just think you should talk to your GM.
She's new, a transfer, heavyset, latina.
(I'm sorry to be blunt. No one wears nametags.)*
That's fine. Go on. What did she do to you?
*Well, it's not so much a certain thing she did.
It's just her energy. No smiles. No "thanks*

*for stopping in." I always leave a tip,
and she says nothing. Once, I even asked
her what her name was. She said, 'Why?"* Oh dear,
that's terrible. *I know.* I thought so too.
*I just don't think she likes her job at all.
It's rubbing off on everyone around her.*

*The crew all talk to me like they're afraid
she'll dock their pay for every cube of chicken
they serve above four ounces. It's absurd!*
Sorry to hear that. I hope you can forgive
her brusqueness as protection of the business.
Still, it's your experience that counts.

I'll call *her* boss and have him talk to her
about how people are our business, too!
I'm sure a one-on-one will do the trick.
I know you said you don't want something free,
but I would feel remiss unless I offered
a little something to express our thanks.

We can talk about the details, but
I'd like to give you my virginity.
I lost it when I was eighteen years old,
watching *Final Destination 2*
with Bryan Young, the first out boy I'd met.
I told him he felt good. I guess he did.

Sincerely, Chipotle

We haven't talked in years. I doubt he'd mind
if I took back the tenderness he plucked
and sent it to you in a FedEx tube.
I'll only need your address and a number
the guy can call you at if something breaks.
I so appreciate your willingness

to talk about such touchy things as sex
and politics. You know, we serve burritos,
but nothing's ever just burritos, is it?
I'll tell you this: each day, I wake at six,
fall back asleep, and wake nine minutes later.
I play this game until I can't afford to.

I talk myself out of malingering,
which may be all that anyone can ask.
I cannot stomach all your grievances,
and then I do. I drink six cups of coffee.
I meet my daily goals. I close your case.
Shut up, please shut up, and come back soon.

Agate

I.

The interstate's particulars have all but evaporated.
A few linger:
my brother's off-key baritone;
a charter bus wobbling in the passing lane;
Agate, Colorado, passing by in seconds;
Wheat Jesus on a strip-mall billboard, his beard
bleeding into the grain.

We've arrived in Kansas, my mother's farm
with its 150 acres and
(thank god) Wi-Fi.

I google "blue agate":
a motherlode
of lakes, floes of white crystal,
lacy irises, cerulean
depths where light sings
its last, mournful notes.

I dream I'm trapped inside a mall kiosk,
hawking agate coasters.

II.

My brother and stepfather go off to shoot.
The Lavender Orpingtons
flock in the chicken yard,
the rooster's red wattle
dangling.
War movies
watch over Grandpa.

The sun sieves through the dilapidated roof
of the rotting barn, dappling the dirt.
A warped piano sleeps behind a sagging sofa

Agate

in the paddocks. I piss in front of them.
Two owls, bisque-white, fly
out the southern gable.
I sneeze and the cows stampede.

III.

Above the surface of a pond, bullfrogs
peek, their eyes golden, their pupils chasms.
My brother and I each command an oar
in the aluminum canoe, cracking jokes,
churning scum.

We say our goodbyes.

We pass Wheat Jesus.

We append "Anal" to the names of RVs:

Anal Bounder.

Anal Zephyr.

Anal Prowler.

Anal Vengeance.

I play a podcast on the possibility of altruism.

Agate passes quickly as before.

Diaristic

Saturday. On my t-shirt, blue moons
in every phase, parentheses within parentheses,
teal moons above them, then white, yellow, orange, rising like chakras
up my belly to my sternum, a full crimson moon glowing just under my throat.

Every day, a periwinkle antidepressant
stills the handsome editor wielding the word *diaristic*
as an impalement artist might wield a throwing knife. I am the target boy,
strapped to a wheel of death plastered with page upon page of my own writing.

I slip from my shackles, strip paper off wood,
make a frock of chicken scratch and dog ears. I don a wig
frizzing with fringe of notebook leaves unbound from their spiral.
I live, and will die, a diarist, collecting days like costume jewelry, dancing

alone in moonlit snow, decked out
in daydreams, diatribes, digressions, drips of coffee.
Line my coffin with my diaries. Lower me into the earth
to write another lifetime with my body, my own unrepeatable language.

This Poem Is a Gift to Myself

First of all, I give you time
enough to drown in
because I know how well you swim.

Then, I give you elation
uncut by fear of its end, a sunset
slow as nectar
trickling down your cheek, every color
saturated and sticky.

I give you the mountains,
which were always yours.

I give you all the best pain
in a sharp, crystalline container
to display on a shelf in your favorite room.

I give you houseguests to admire the shelf.
I give you a feather duster and the soft glow of a lamp.
I give you a cat to leap onto the shelf with a *thunk*.

I give you the cat's paw
poking the crystal closer and closer to the edge.

I give you permission to be the crystal
and permission to be the cat.

A Brief History of the Denver Scrabble Club

When the Cherry Creek-adjacent
church's basement raised the rent,
we took our cues from Noah's Ark.
QUAD begat QUADRUPED.
KINK begat KINKAJOU.
We landed at the Village Inn
on COLORADO (much like TEXAS
and ALASKA, a playable word,
though rarely played). Six years since,
our waitrons have been fairly tipped.
The one who still refuses service
smiles politely as I pass
to hit the jakes. The dictionary
now boasts TWERK and FRENEMY.

Tonight, the theme is fireworks.
The winning word: KABLOOEY, though
POTASSIUM is laudable,
shooting upwards from the UM.
Outside, explosions punctuate
our plays. FEMINAZI stems
out of an unassuming FEM.
Bizarro twin of NONISSUE,
UNSONSIE cleaves a game in two.
Our attendees: retirees,
divorcees, all devotees
to some degree. An easy JEEZ
collides with an advanced HAFIZ.
We log our scores. The booms subside.
I, Director, hand out prizes:
Pop Rocks, an American flag.
We pay no dues or entry fees.

We hope to draw a blank or two,
to rise in rank, to recognize
a phony or play one for the books,

to keep our cool, to never cry
again. *It's just a game,* we lie
to newbs and victims of our routs.
An expert (name omitted here)
once overturned a table over
ORGANDY, spelled with a Y,
not, as he swore, with an I-E
(both are valid, for the record),
and took a two-yearlong hiatus.
We hope our families don't hate us
for our neglect of greater talents.
We hope our spirits, like our racks,
demonstrate both strength and balance.

Between *Home* and *Sexual*

—after Tony Hoagland

Summer, and the gays remember
                                we hate clothes.
Tan lines disappear. Man-
scaped creatures burn along the river-
banks where lovers make deposits
and bounce. We relearn the warmth
of underwater frottage, the allover kiss
of stubble, the various intrusions of sand.

On our newsfeeds, we are shown
a group of frat brothers in Mississippi
(not the first) posing
in front of an Emmett Till memorial
with AR-15s, rosy cheeks, white smiles,
                                fingers on triggers,
two decades into our twenty-first
and probably last century.

It's my birthday. I can't help
but heed the alerts and Love
the stream of friendship
flowing down my Face-
book wall, each pleasantry drifting

between reports from the border camps.
I know the former, slowly, insidiously,
wears away the latter.
                            Tony, you called it a ditch

running between *home* and *sexual*,
into which our hawkish legislators stumbled
during the Defense hearings.
You undershot—it's a river

Between Home *and* Sexual

we must cross to keep on living.
Bodies wash up on both sides,
bloated, beaten, barely recognizable.

It's easy to forget
hatred never stops coming for any of us.
But hatred never stops coming for any of us.

Still summer, still the day I was born,
and here by the river,
my fellow man is naked,

pale, and, for the moment, safe
as so many aren't. Soon,
we will swim back into the water
and together, hopefully, make it back to shore.

A Note about the Author

Photo courtesy of Alex Dean, © 2020

James Phillip Davis was born on a U.S. Army base in Nuremburg, Germany, in 1985 and grew up in Colorado Springs, CO. He has a BA in French from the University of Houston and an MFA in Creative Writing from the University of Florida. He has worked in marketing and instructional design for a major restaurant chain and as a high school speech-and-debate coach. His poems have appeared in two installments of the *Best New Poets* anthology (2011 & 2019), as well as numerous print and online journals, including *American Literary Review, Copper Nickel, The Gay & Lesbian Review,* and *32 Poems*. When not writing, he plays tournament Scrabble and is consistently ranked among the top 100 players in North America.

A Note About the Anthony Hecht Poetry Prize

The Anthony Hecht Poetry Prize was inaugurated in 2005 and is awarded on an annual basis to the best first or second collection of poems submitted.

FIRST ANNUAL HECHT PRIZE
Judge: J. D. McClatchy
Winner: Morrie Creech, *Field Knowledge*

SECOND ANNUAL HECHT PRIZE
Judge: Mary Jo Salter
Winner: Erica Dawson, *Big-Eyed Afraid*

THIRD ANNUAL HECHT PRIZE
Judge: Richard Wilbur
Winner: Rose Kelleher, *Bundle o' Tinder*

FOURTH ANNUAL HECHT PRIZE
Judge: Alan Shapiro
Winner: Carrie Jerrell, *After the Revival*

FIFTH ANNUAL HECHT PRIZE
Judge: Rosanna Warren
Winner: Matthew Ladd, *The Book of Emblems*

SIXTH ANNUAL HECHT PRIZE
Judge: James Fenton
Winner: Mark Kraushaar, *The Uncertainty Principle*

SEVENTH ANNUAL HECHT PRIZE
Judge: Mark Strand
Winner: Chris Andrews, *Lime Green Chair*

EIGHTH ANNUAL HECHT PRIZE
Judge: Charles Simic
Winner: Shelley Puhak, *Guinevere in Baltimore*

A Note About the Anthony Hecht Poetry Prize

NINTH ANNUAL HECHT PRIZE
Judge: Heather McHugh
Winner: Geoffrey Brock, *Voices Bright Flags*

TENTH ANNUAL HECHT PRIZE
Judge: Anthony Thwaite
Winner: Jaimee Hills, *How to Avoid Speaking*

ELEVENTH ANNUAL HECHT PRIZE
Judge: Eavan Boland
Winner: Austin Allen, *Pleasures of the Game*

TWELFTH ANNUAL HECHT PRIZE
Judge: Gjertrud Schnackenberg
Winner: Mike White, *Addendum to a Miracle*

THIRTEENTH ANNUAL HECHT PRIZE
Judge: Andrew Motion
Winner: Christopher Cessac, *The Youngest Ocean*

FOURTEENTH ANNUAL HECHT PRIZE
Judge: Charles Wright
Winner: Katherine Hollander, *My German Dictionary*

FIFTEENTH ANNUAL HECHT PRIZE
Judge: Ed Hirsch
Winner: James Davis, *Club Q*

Other Books from Waywiser

POETRY

Austin Allen, *Pleasures of the Game*
Al Alvarez, *New & Selected Poems*
Chris Andrews, *Lime Green Chair*
Audrey Bohanan, *Any Keep or Contour*
George Bradley, *A Few of Her Secrets*
Geoffrey Brock, *Voices Bright Flags*
Christopher Cessac, *The Youngest Ocean*
Robert Conquest, *Blokelore & Blokesongs*
Robert Conquest, *Collected Poems*
Robert Conquest, *Penultimata*
Morri Creech, *Blue Rooms*
Morri Creech, *Field Knowledge*
Morri Creech, *The Sleep of Reason*
Peter Dale, *One Another*
Erica Dawson, *Big-Eyed Afraid*
B. H. Fairchild, *The Art of the Lathe*
David Ferry, *On This Side of the River: Selected Poems*
Daniel Groves & Greg Williamson, eds., *Jiggery-Pokery Semicentennial*
Jeffrey Harrison, *The Names of Things: New & Selected Poems*
Joseph Harrison, *Identity Theft*
Joseph Harrison, *Shakespeare's Horse*
Joseph Harrison, *Someone Else's Name*
Joseph Harrison, *Sometimes I Dream That I Am Not Walt Whitman*
Joseph Harrison, ed., *The Hecht Prize Anthology, 2005-2009*
Anthony Hecht, *Collected Later Poems*
Anthony Hecht, *The Darkness and the Light*
Jaimee Hills, *How to Avoid Speaking*
Katherine Hollander, *My German Dictionary*
Hilary S. Jacqmin, *Missing Persons*
Carrie Jerrell, *After the Revival*
Stephen Kampa, *Articulate as Rain*
Stephen Kampa, *Bachelor Pad*
Rose Kelleher, *Bundle o' Tinder*
Mark Kraushaar, *The Uncertainty Principle*
Matthew Ladd, *The Book of Emblems*
J. D. McClatchy, *Plundered Hearts: New and Selected Poems*
Dora Malech, *Shore Ordered Ocean*
Jérôme Luc Martin, *The Gardening Fires: Sonnets and Fragments*
Eric McHenry, *Odd Evening*
Eric McHenry, *Potscrubber Lullabies*
Eric McHenry and Nicholas Garland, *Mommy Daddy Evan Sage*
Timothy Murphy, *Very Far North*
Ian Parks, *Shell Island*
V. Penelope Pelizzon, *Whose Flesh is Flame, Whose Bone is Time*
Chris Preddle, *Cattle Console Him*

Other Books from Waywiser

Shelley Puhak, *Guinevere in Baltimore*
Christopher Ricks, ed., *Joining Music with Reason:*
34 Poets, British and American, Oxford 2004-2009
Daniel Rifenburgh, *Advent*
Mary Jo Salter, *It's Hard to Say: Selected Poems*
W. D. Snodgrass, *Not for Specialists: New & Selected Poems*
Mark Strand, *Almost Invisible*
Mark Strand, *Blizzard of One*
Bradford Gray Telford, *Perfect Hurt*
Matthew Thorburn, *This Time Tomorrow*
Cody Walker, *Shuffle and Breakdown*
Cody Walker, *The Self-Styled No-Child*
Cody Walker, *The Trumpiad*
Deborah Warren, *The Size of Happiness*
Clive Watkins, *Already the Flames*
Clive Watkins, *Jigsaw*
Richard Wilbur, *Anterooms*
Richard Wilbur, *Mayflies*
Richard Wilbur, *Collected Poems 1943-2004*
Norman Williams, *One Unblinking Eye*
Greg Williamson, *A Most Marvelous Piece of Luck*
Greg Williamson, *The Hole Story of Kirby the Sneak and Arlo the True*
Stephen Yenser, *Stone Fruit*

FICTION
Gregory Heath, *The Entire Animal*
Mary Elizabeth Pope, *Divining Venus*
K. M. Ross, *The Blinding Walk*
Gabriel Roth, *The Unknowns**
Matthew Yorke, *Chancing It*

ILLUSTRATED
Nicholas Garland, *I wish ...*
Eric McHenry and Nicholas Garland, *Mommy Daddy Evan Sage*
Greg Williamson, *The Hole Story of Kirby the Sneak and Arlo the True*

NON-FICTION
Neil Berry, *Articles of Faith: The Story of British Intellectual Journalism*
Irving Feldman, *Usable Truths: Aphorisms & Observations*
Mark Ford, *A Driftwood Altar: Essays and Reviews*
Philip Hoy, ed., *A Bountiful Harvest:*
The Correspondence of Anthony Hecht and William L. MacDonald
Richard Wollheim, *Germs: A Memoir of Childhood*

* Co-published with Picador